THE E-COMMERCE BOOKLET

Oliver Petrik

This booklet is dedicated to those individuals who grind endlessly and work for their own success. They take the sole responsibility for themselves, their community, and family. Those who don't complain, instead they only execute. They don't give up. Keep winning!

INTRODUCTION

It seems like every single day you have ads constantly reaching you on YouTube and other platforms about some guy that had success with e-commerce or a variation of some sort of online business. It could be a course, book, store, literally anything, but it's constantly there in your face, and it's probably just plain annoying to you. Well, the real reason behind this is most of these "annoying" people are making lots of money online and monetizing you the "consumer" or "viewer" by driving traffic and attention to whatever they are selling. If you want to become the "annoying" person that makes money completely online and from the privacy of your own home, well this booklet is the perfect thing for you. Think of this booklet as a cheat sheet. You will acquire important knowledge that takes many years to gather. It will either help you get started or expand!

Remember this "You can accomplish anything you can possibly dream of as long as you put in the work required for the dream, and the rest will be put into place automatically by the universe." - Oliver Petrik

Remember this "Winners don't hate on other winners, they only support other winners. The weak little bitches in society aka lazy, unmotivated people, are the ones that hate and bitch about everything." - Oliver Petrik

Below are some things you can personally implement to boost/start your e-commerce sales. These things must be used constantly and accurately for every product or item on any platform that you choose to sell on.

- You must offer free shipping on all your products.
- You must take excellent photos of your products.
- You must have accurate product descriptions and details
- You must ship out any sales within 1 business day.
- You must answer any questions or concerns, from of any actual or potential customers both fast and adequately.
- You must have the proper equipment and supplies at all times (I will further explain this later on)
- Lastly, you must be extremely positive, and you must continue to think big 25/8.

You decide your own income in the field of e-commerce, the more you work, the more you make! It's that simple.

CONTENTS

WHAT DO YOU NEED
TO GET STARTED?

You are probably wondering what you need to purchase to get started. I will explain what you need to get started, while also minimizing start-up costs. I will include some exact supplies to help you out. If you read this booklet a while after it was published, just disregard those exact products, but purchase the same type of items and the same amount as described. A disclaimer: I have no connection with neither those products nor the sellers of those products.

Keep all your receipts for anything you purchase for your business. It doesn't matter whether you think you will make enough income to where you have to pay taxes or not. You can't predict the future, if you don't keep your receipts you should just forget e-commerce. Discarding receipts will mess up your taxes and mess up your money while limiting your potential.

You will need a postage scale. This will save you lots of money. For example, let's say you have an item that sold that weighs 4oz if you purchase a shipping label for 6oz- this alone will cost you more and cut your profits. In the long term, you are committing financial suicide if you don't purchase a scale. I recommend purchasing a postage scale with a maximum weight of 20-30lbs or as high as the items you think you will be selling weigh. You can buy a decent scale on either eBay or Amazon for less than 10 dollars. Do yourself a favor and start the right way and buy one right now. The second you finish this booklet or even this paragraph go order one. There's a scale on eBay right now, that's listed for $8.99 with free shipping. The title of the item is Digital Weigh Packaging Shipping Postal Scale LCD Display 10kg/0.5g 22lb White. Again, this item and the seller both have no connection with me whatsoever.

If you just ordered a scale Congratulations', that's the first step to e-commerce success! I wish you luck and lots of prosperity.

You will need packaging tape. This is cheap and also be purchased on either eBay or Amazon for cheap. Just shop around and buy the cheapest one. Not the one with the cheapest price, instead purchase the one with the cheapest per roll or unit price. This is how the successful think, they think long term, they don't do temporary fixes. Order enough rolls for your business plus a little more. Here's some tape you can purchase; Tape King Clear Packing Tape 3 Inch Wide (Case of 24 Rolls) - 60 Yards Per Refill Roll, (2.7mil Thick) Strong Sealing Adhesive Industrial Depot Tapes for Moving, Packaging, Shipping, Office & Storage. (It's on amazon)

You will need scissors. Just go to the dollar store or dollar general or something similar to that. I don't have an exact recommendation for scissors.

You will need a printer and paper. I don't have an exact recommendation for a printer. Shop around and look for fair priced ink-efficient printers.

You will need a car if you don't have one. If you don't have a car, you must be living in a location with some sort of good public transportation. You will need transportation to go to the post office and to purchase inventory and supplies.

You will need a personal computer with a decent internet connection. I'm sure most of you have a car and also a laptop. The computer controls your whole business. The internet supplies your computer with the whole world.

You will need a smartphone with data. This will help you look up the product values instantly, and you will be taking photos with your phone. Again, I'm sure most of you have this, but I want to lay out the foundation for success, just in case.

Note: you can take photos of your products with whatever you wish; a phone, or camera, etc.

You will need some sort of background to make your listing look more professional. You can use anything pretty much. I use two project display boards (two tri-fold poster boards). Because you need two. One for the bottom and one for the background. Here's something you can purchase; Elmer's Tri-Fold Display Board, White, 14x22 Inch. This is crucial to the success of your e-commerce business and will in return generate you lots of additional sales.

You will need Goo Off Heavy Duty (I will cover this later). It removes things such as sharpie marks from most tags. Search for Goo Off Heavy Duty. You can purchase this almost anywhere, just order it online. Do this, along with the other required supplies that you currently don't have.

You will need a ruler or preferably a measuring tape. This is crucial to your success. Without a ruler or measuring tape, you can't measure your products. That would be terrible.

You will need a lint roller to clean products such as clothing.

You will need different sizes of boxes and envelopes, solely depending on the items you sell. Always use envelopes rather than boxes if possible- it is much cheaper to ship as they are lighter. Order boxes from your local post office. The USPS offers many boxes for free online, get all types and sizes. You never know what you will need one day. Buy supplies online, if you would like to do so. Or even check local recycling dumpsters and get some for free. Be sure to get permission before doing so.

Remember "Reduce, Reuse, Recycle". I buy my polybag envelopes directly from eBay shipping supplies. (14.5" x 18.5" No padding) I buy other regular envelopes from Sam's Club online. (10"x 13" Clasp Envelopes) You can even ask family and friends for boxes and envelopes if they order a lot online. Just be sure to remove any previous shipping labels, you want to protect their privacy.

This is all you "need". However, you could purchase things like professional lighting, but that doesn't do anything but drive up overall costs thus cutting profits. All of these items are extremely simple, but I wish I had a guide like this to follow when I started e-commerce. That would have sped up the process. Good luck finding another e-commerce guide that tells you about Goo-Off. Others won't tell you the little secrets, they will tell you the things that are pretty much common knowledge. It's simple, but it will enable you to sell any items that are either in the original packaging or that just have the tags, as new in many cases.

Now that we established the boring foundation, let's get started! Let's make some money!

HOW TO RAISE CAPITAL?

How do you raise capital? The real answer is you don't have to at all. The reason is that the average household has already over $3,000 of items that they do not use. That's pretty much 3 free grand. I recommend selling all of the items that are currently collecting dust in your home first. After you sell all or some of these items, then finally go out and purchase some inventory. Depending on what platform you opt to sell on and the scale you wish to reach, you will need a small amount of cash to cover a variety of things, including shipping costs, items returns and replacements, inventory cost, and all of the supplies I previously mentioned.

HOW TO SOURCE INVENTORY AND PRICE ITEMS?

Sourcing... This is the most important section of this entire booklet, the main aspect that will decide your income and also your profit margins. But remember this, the more you source, the more you make. It's the same as the more you work, the more you make. There are multiple ways you can source or different business models including free sections, thrifting, wholesale, and retail arbitrage. I will explain these later in this chapter. You want to choose the business model that best fits your needs, wants, and honest commitment.

Profit Calculators

For eBay, use an online eBay profit calculator for all products. (Easy)

For Amazon, use the Amazon app for all products. (Easy)

For other platforms, it varies but usually, profit calculators are built into the app. (Very easy)

Free Sections

The free section is a great business model for anyone that wishes to do e-commerce part-time due to other time commitments. And the best part is it costs absolutely nothing. Yes, nothing.

All you have to do is check local selling sites such as Facebook Marketplace and Craigslist for free items, and then you sell them. Look them up before you agree to meet with people. Also, be safe! I wouldn't recommend picking up something like a couch or a large recliner chair unless you plan to sell them locally. These items will be very hard to ship, and they aren't typically worth your time. If you choose to utilize and enact this business model, check every day for new items on multiple local sites, and simply sell them. Or you could utilize this business model in addition to another. It's free money! No risk, just reward! If something doesn't sell quickly, simply donate it. (Get the tax write-off)

Thrifting/Used Sourcing

Thrifting is a great business model for anyone who wishes to have extremely high profit margins, and who has little to no time commitments. Thrifting is very common for consumers, not just resellers. The real reason why most of society has little to nothing financially is that they consume much too much and produce too little. You get paid for what you offer to the market. Thrifting is like therapy to me, it always makes me happy, because of the high-profit margins! It's similar to treasure hunting. For this business model, all you have to do is check out local thrift stores, and look up interesting looking items, buy and sell them, and then repeat... Look for anything in its original packaging or simply items with tags. You can go to the salvation army, goodwill, or whatever thrift stores are nearest to you. The best thrift stores tend to be the smaller charity-based ones, not the big national ones like Goodwill and the Salvation army. However, I can't mention any small local charity thrift shops because they are completely dependent on location, and they typically only have one location.

My strategy for thrifting is always getting a shopping cart first thing when you enter the building, then go look for that gold.

Put everything you potentially may want to sell in your shopping cart and then look them up after. This way other customers or in my eyes "enemies" cannot take your profits from you. Check for electronics, video games, clothes, kitchenware, books, DVDs, toys, picture frames, shoes, or simply whatever in that store draws your attention and rings the $$$$ bell in your brain. You should see me in thrift stores. I'm like a little kid in a candy store, I run around and throw everything in my cart. People in thrift stores will often ask you if you purchase lots of items at once, "what are you going to do with all the items". Simply tell them, they are gifts for my kids, grandkids, cousins, brother, sister, etc. I get asked this almost every single time I am in a thrift store due to my frequent visits to the same local locations. Be sure to keep your answer the same exactly always, as it will automatically become natural and much less awkward. You can scan UPCs on items in thrift stores if they have one, if they don't have UPCs you can simply research the item's value on whatever platform you plan to sell it on. **Look for both sold and active items. Look for both sold and active items. Look for both sold and active items. Look for both sold and active items. Look for both sold and active items. Look for both sold and active items. Look for both sold and active items.** eBay and many other selling platforms have a sold filter, Amazon does not but they have an Amazon seller app that is completely free. The Amazon seller app allows you to research items and their potential profit margins.

Once you have checked the sold items, also check the active (currently listed) items. For example, let's say you have a blanket and it previously sold for $50, there may be one currently listed for $40. So, the value of that item for you is only $40, not $50, simply because of your competition. Only purchase items if you KNOW you can make a nice PROFIT OFF THEM AND MORE IMPORTANTLY FAST. E-commerce is less about profit margins and more about volume. I would rather sell 10 items each day making $10 profit each one (total of $100), than 5 items each day making $12 profit each (total of $60). The cheaper your price is, the higher the items demand will be! But be careful, you do not want to completely ruin the item. For example, if an item sells for $50, and you list it for $20, you are completely killing that item. Instead, try listing it for $48 or $49 and if it doesn't sell for a while, then drop the price over time. This will keep that item's value constant for a long period of time, and this will benefit you in the long run. For example, I have sold some of the same items many times. If I would have undercut the price massively, I would have completely destroyed the market for myself. Massively undercutting prices is financial suicide. Be careful with thrift stores - sometimes products are damaged, broken, or destroyed. Don't buy these at all. However, sometimes you will get home and you will realize that one of the items is damaged. If you paid a small amount, just throw it away or donate it. You don't want to sell damaged items because they will end up hurting your reputation and prestige. If you notice only a slight flaw with an item, just be sure to take pictures of the flaw and put them in your listing in addition to the regular photos, and also describe it well and adequately in the description. This will ensure that you receive lots of positive feedback on whatever platform you choose to sell on. (I will discuss some of the major platforms later)

The more feedback you have and the better your feedback is, the more a potential buyer is to purchase your products. Feedback is crucial to your e-commerce success. Do everything in your power to maintain at least 99% percent feedback or a 5-star rating depending on the platform. The only downside with thrifting is you cannot return any items to the store. With retail arbitrage (another e-commerce business model) you can return up to a certain amount depending on the store you purchase items from. It is still a low risk, high return business model because you are paying little to nothing for each item, and you will be looking up the sold and active listings while you are in the store, before you purchase those items. With thrifting, you will want to travel to "richer" areas to source because they usually get better items than "poorer" areas. The "rich" people tend to be lazy (middle-class housewives) and they just want to get rid of stuff, so those thrift shops end up with higher quality products much more frequently. Some thrift store locations (even in the same company) have ridiculous prices. Go to the cheapest ones in your area. You will want to create either a word document or just simply write on a piece of paper, regarding when are the discount days at your local thrift stores. This will further increase your profits. However, don't wait to snag a good item until the discount day. If you observe a good profitable item, just purchase it. Profit is profit, and that item may sell before the discount day! I have sold many items within a few minutes after listing it. When thrifting lookout for brand name items, it doesn't matter what type of item they are. For example, Nintendo, Xbox, Sony, Ralph Lauren Polo, Louis Vuitton, Lululemon, Disney, etc. I haven't found Louis Vuitton thrifting, but I know people that have! That's a total gold mine, but make sure it is authentic and be sure to research it before you purchase it. Keep in mind that you can get banned or suspended for selling counterfeit goods.

Besides just sourcing from thrift stores, I highly recommend garage sales, estate sales, flea markets, pawnshops, antique stores, etc. Garage sales usually have higher profit margins than thrift stores because the "idiots" don't know what their items are worth, or they are simply too lazy to sell them online. As harsh as it sounds, I like to call them idiots, because most of the garage sale hosts aren't, in fact, rich, and even worse they work stupid jobs. But take advantage of garage sales, you can make serious money off people's laziness and stupidity. Work smarter, not harder. You can also source used items from Facebook Marketplace and other online local platforms, but this way you will have to pay for the items. This is a good method, again most people are lazy and stupid, and just want to get rid of stuff. Don't rush sourcing, the more time you put into researching and inspecting your items, the more profit you will make! A decent thrift store should take you over an hour, just searching for good profitable items, then inspecting them, and then the final purchasing of the items. I recommend you source at least once a week but do it for the whole day! Go to sleep early the previous night and wake up around 8 am (or an hour before the first thrift store you want to go to opens). Be sure the next stores you wish to go to are open also. Be there at the thrift store, the second the dang place opens! This will massively increase your profits because you are now time efficient. You will end up getting much better items, and at the same time much faster. Fewer customers, less traffic, less problems and complications. Don't stop sourcing until you have been to at least 3-5 stores or sources. Go to 10+ stores if you can. Be sure to make a document of all the stores you plan to travel to, the night before, and put them in order by location. (use Google Maps or MapQuest) This will make you the queen or king of time. Make sure you bring that document whether it is online on your phone, or just a piece of paper with you. If you have it online, you can simply put your destinations in one by one into Google Maps. Community-wide garage sales are a gold mine. Attend these in your area as much as possible! Look for NEW ITEMS IN THE PACKAGE OR WITH THE TAGS, and for NAME BRANDS! Name brands with the tags will go for even more! I wouldn't recommend getting lesser-known brands at all. But do your research by looking everything up! **Look everything up! Look everything up!** If you skip this step, as some beginners do, you will almost always fail. Once you get more experienced like me, you won't have to look up each item, simply for the reason that you will have already sold some of the items, therefore you already know their value, and how fast or slow the items will sell.

Retail Arbitrage

Retail Arbitrage is my favorite e-commerce business model. The reason is that you are selling only new items, but a high quantity of the same item. Therefore, you only have to create one listing for the product, but you then change the quantity. Retail arbitrage is the process of buying products in retail stores and then, of course, selling them for a profit online. This is a very

common business model for many resellers nowadays. You literally go around retail stores and scan the UPC codes with either
the eBay or Amazon app, and then you sell them. If you choose to
sell on a platform without a UPC scanner, you can simply just
search for the item manually. You want to search for both sold
and listed items, the same as with thrifting. Check the clearance
section! Check the clearance section! Walk around the store and
look for sales! Look for yellow tags (the sale tag color most of the
time). Similarly, to thrifting, you want to get a shopping cart the
moment you walk into the store. Check for video games, electronics, clothing, toys, etc. (anything that is on sale). Most of the
time if the item is not on sale, you will not be able to make a decent enough profit on it. (In some cases, you will lose money)
Good retail stores include, but are not limited to; Target, Walmart, Ross, Marshalls. The best thing with the retail arbitrage
business model is that you can return the items if they don't sell.
Of course, you want to check the return and refund policies at
your store. That is another reason why it is vitally important to
keep all your receipts! Keep your retail arbitrage receipts separ-
ated from your thrift store receipts. Thrift store receipts are only
useful for tax purposes and bookkeeping. Retail Arbitrage receipts are useful for returns, and tax purposes and bookkeeping.
Return unsold items to different locations. For example, if you
buy 5 video games at Walmart, try returning 3 video games at
one Walmart location, and then go to another Walmart location
and return 2 more. Also, be sure to pay with cash if you can and
don't use any rewards programs for your retail arbitrage pur-
chases. This way, the retail stores will have a much harder time
tracking how many returns you have made. Keep this in mind,
some retail stores offer a return policy, but they limit you to a
certain amount in a certain time frame. That being said, you
should only be purchasing items that make you a nice profit (at
least 1.5-2x ROI). The items you purchase should also be able to
sell fast. The Amazon seller app gives you a sales ranking for each
product. ROI and length of turnover are almost completely dependent on your research. If an item you have purchased doesn't

sell after a week or two, drop the price slowly and consistently until it sells. (Make sure you are still making a profit off it whether it will be just $1 or $100). Profit is profit. If it doesn't sell by the day before the return policy expires, return it. Consistently dropping the price over time, will get you more sales and it will also result in you having to conduct fewer returns, but be sure you are still making a profit. Now go out and get some items from local retail stores!

Wholesale

There are many different variations of the wholesale business model. The variation that I am most familiar with I will explain. There are other variations, that I am not that experienced with, so I will not cover those variations. eBay will be your best friend for the wholesale business model. All you have to do is look on eBay for lots (bulk items), and then look them up and see if you can make a profit off them. For example, some sellers sell lots of Lego sets brand new. They will sell like 5-25 sets in one listing. Usually you can pick up the lot for a cheaper price than they individually go for, and then you can sell them individually on eBay or Amazon, or whatever platform you choose. Be careful you will have to factor in the shipping cost that you will have to pay to ship each item. I previously mentioned you will be offering free shipping on all your product listings. Use the profit calculator mentioned above for the platform you choose. You can sell the individual items on the platform you purchase them or on another platform. It doesn't matter as long as you are making a profit.

HOW TO FIND YOUR NICHE?

How to Find your eCommerce Niche? Your niche will be determined by whatever you personally have the most experience in, and also your preferred sourcing locations. What I mean by this is, if you have experience in athletic clothing then always look for athletic clothing. If you have experience in video games, then always look for video games. That being said, you want to diversify your business and sell different categories of items and also you want to sell on multiple platforms. (I will cover the different major platforms later) Also, you will find a trend of very frequent profitable items within your preferred sourcing locations. What I mean by this is, one of your frequented stores may always have lots of profitable video games. So, your niche will become video games automatically. You want a constant source of inventory. You should be posting at least 5-10 product listings per day if you want to take e-commerce semi-seriously.

STOCKING UP ON INVENTORY?

You want to stock up inventory well in advance of the major holidays and seasons. The main holiday that will drive your sales is, of course, the entire Christmas season! These holiday sales run from approximately the beginning of October through the middle of January after the New Year. However, it is completely dependent on the types of products you sell and your niche! Black Friday is a good day to run a massive sale on all your products. If you don't already know, Black Friday is always the Friday following Thanksgiving. I recommend running a storewide sale for at least the day before which is Thanksgiving, and also for the day after. Preferably you run a storewide sale for that whole week until Tuesday, which is the day after Cyber Monday. Super Saturday is another day that gets lots of sales. I run a storewide sale from the middle of November until the middle of January to cover this whole shopping period or frenzy. Just be sure to stock up plenty of inventory during the months leading up to it. You also want to consistently add lots of inventory during this period to further boost your sales. Pretty much you just have to make sure you have ample inventory for the upcoming seasons and major holidays. The list of major holidays includes all of these but is not limited to St. Patrick's Day, Easter, Mother's Day, Father's Day, the Fourth of July, Halloween, Hanukkah, Valentine's Day, New Year's, and Christmas. This strategy works by far the best if you seek out some holiday-specific inventory well before the upcoming holiday, whatever it may be. Typically, you can also price those holiday-specific items before the related holiday a little bit higher. Just be sure to sell any seasonal items before the related holiday, because the market price will massively decrease immediately after the holiday.

PREPARING/ PREPPING INVENTORY

This step is crucial to e-commerce success and this process will increase your sales if you take the time to do it properly. It's pretty self-explanatory, but I will cover it. Preparing and prepping inventory varies for different categories of products. Be sure you remove any existing price tags; this is very very important. You do not want potential customers knowing the retail price. If a product only has a sharpie mark on a tag or something similar, I recommend buying Goo Off Heavy Duty (previously mentioned) so you can remove it easily and efficiently. If you are selling clothing be sure to wash, clean, and iron them if necessary, before listing the product. If the clothing is still new with the tags, don't just list it as is. For this step of the process pretty much, just clean your products and also remove any tags from them. You can also use a lint roller to make your items appear a little cleaner. All these very simple steps will ensure that you boost your sales.

THE BEST-SELLING PLATFORMS!

The platform you choose to sell on will be dependent on the categories of items you plan to sell. Some platforms are better than others for different categories of products. Some platforms even command a higher price for the same item than others. This makes it very important for you to check the price on multiple platforms. You, of course, want to list where you can sell an item for the most money, and you also want to be sure to sell it pretty fast. You can also cross-list your items on multiple platforms, but this is risky depending on your situation. If you work a full-time job or go to college or do something else that takes a lot of your focus away, I do not recommend cross-listing then. If you decide to cross-list or sell the same item on multiple platforms at the same time, you must make sure you can delete the item whenever it sells immediately, on the platform(s) that it hasn't sold yet on. This is the reason why I don't suggest doing this if you do something else besides e-commerce, which is very time-consuming. The majority of successful e-commerce sellers sell their products on multiple platforms. Because you don't want all your eggs in one basket. Some sellers cross-list, some don't. Cross-listing is entirely up to you. Most successful sellers have their favorite platforms to sell on, you can't sell on too many at once. It is too time-consuming. Stick with 2-3 platforms and grow on those. Always send potential buyers offers as frequently as possible. Be sure to do this multiple times every single day! Whatever platform you want to sell on, it doesn't matter, try to sell as many items that weigh under a pound. This will increase your profit margins tremendously. Change your prices on eBay or any platform you use, every day if possible. Keep your prices the lowest on that platform, this will tremendously increase your sales. Many new sellers under or overprice products. You want to be the cheapest by about 5% off the next cheapest listing of the same item, don't purchase any inventory that you can't manage to do that with, and still make a good profit.

Platform #1 eBay

eBay is the #1 platform to sell any used or vintage items on. It is also great for any new items! I sell the majority of my items on eBay. Amazon is better if you have lots of new items. If you choose to sell on eBay, you get paid through PayPal instantly after the sale. (within seconds after the sale) Amazon takes approximately 2 weeks after the sale for you to receive your money. The main benefit of selling on Amazon is it is by far the largest e-commerce site in terms of traffic and overall sales.

I recommend selling on both eBay and Amazon, and maybe another site like Mercari or Poshmark. If you choose to sell on eBay and take it seriously, you should consider an eBay store sub-scription. They run from $4.95 a month to $2,999.95 a month. The subscription you choose should solely depend on the volume of items you have to sell. You get many benefits with having a eBay store subscription. All of the benefits vary from plan to plan. You get a certain number of free listings each month ranging from 100-100,000. This will save you lots of money, as long as you have a decent number of items. All eBay listings renew every 30 days. So, try to sell items within those 30 days. So, if you have at least 50 items, I recommend getting a store subscription. You get other nice benefits including Terapeak research (good for pricing and researching items), and eBay shipping supply coupons. I recom-mend promoting all of your listings at the trending rate on eBay. This will boost you in the search results. It will cut down your margins a little bit, but you can't count a margin if it hasn't sold yet and promoting your listings will generate you more sales. If you are selling a very popular item such as an Xbox One, I recommend that you don't promote at the trending rate and that you just promote it at a 1% rate. These items are fast to sell if you are the cheapest on the market. You always want to list items ensuring that they are the cheapest price on the market (platform) you are selling on. When selling on eBay use the eBay profit calculator (previously mentioned) - this is crucial. Feedback and meeting high performance standards are very important to get lots of sales on eBay. You want to eventually become a top-rated seller. I am a top-rated seller myself. To become a top-rated seller, you have to meet certain performance standards. You can read about the exact benefits and criteria to become a top-rated seller on eBay's website. Currently, to qualify you need: An eBay account that's been active for at least 90 days, A late shipment rate less than or equal to 3%, and five or fewer late shipments, Tracking uploaded within your stated handling time, and carrier validation for 95% of transactions to US buyers, Cases closed without seller resolution less than or equal to 0.3%, and two or fewer cases, A defect rate less than or equal to 0.5%, with three or fewer defects from unique buyers, 100 or more transactions and $1,000 in sales during the last 12 months with US buyers. All of this is very easy to do! You have to wait 90 days for the first requirement. For the second requirement, all you have to do is send out your packages on time (this depends on the handling time you previously set before the sale). Again, I recommend offering free shipping and one business day handling time for all items. This alone will boost your sales. The third requirement is automatically fulfilled if you purchase your shipping labels on eBay, and you definitely should. (As long as you order and print the label on time) The fourth and fifth requirements are related to cases or problems, just avoid these at all costs. Be reliable and honest at all times. If you aren't reliable and honest, this will hurt your feedback and also your performance rating. You could also be banned from eBay. This will result in a loss of sales. The last requirement has to do with sales and transactions, just sell as much as possible!

The sales requirement that is needed to become a top-rated seller is manageable for anyone. eBay charges you many fees: 10% on most items for selling the item, 3% PayPal fee +$.30 for each transaction, plus whatever your promoted listing ad rate is. Be aware of all these fees. You should strive for an average sales price of $20+ on eBay eventually. If you choose to sell on eBay, do not opt into the global shipping program. (It usually automatically opts each listing into it, be sure to uncheck the box and offer international shipping yourself) By shipping your items internationally by yourself on eBay, you will be increasing your profits on any of those sales. Instead of eBay making the money on it, you are. Always enter the actual product weight on each listing, you can put it slightly higher if you would like, but not too much higher. For example, if an item weighs 4oz, you could put 6oz, but don't put 2lbs. When weighing items, be sure to factor in the packaged weight. Boxes and envelopes add weight to the item. You should use USPS first class and priority mail the majority of the time if you live in the United States. First Class mail is for items under 16oz or 1lb. Priority mail is available for almost any weight. Media mail is good if you are shipping any type of media, and it is cheaper than priority or First-Class mail, but it is slower. Your preferred shipping methods solely depend on where you live, where the buyer lives, and on the item, etc.

I do not recommend doing any auctions at all. I don't have auctions on any of my listings. The reason is, you have to wait for a certain duration for the auction to end. This massively extends your inventory turnover period and reduces the compounding of your business's cash flow. In simpler words, it messes up your business! Get lots of feedback as soon as possible! Even if you lose a small amount on a few items at the beginning (anything less than $1.00) your future sales potential exponentially increases. Don't be scared to lose in the beginning, to gain more in the future. This will speed up the process of you becoming a top-rated seller. However, I only recommend that you do this if the item hasn't sold for a good length of time. Let's say at least a month. Be sure to limit your losses, but some minor ones aren't necessarily bad at the start. Even I lost some money at the beginning, but this was done on purpose only to increase my feedback rating much faster, and it later expanded my sales and made me a top-rated seller much faster. Feedback is everything on eBay! Another way to get feedback fast is to just buy products you actually need anyway on eBay. You get feedback most of the time if the seller is reputable. Check their feedback. If it is high (500+), there is a good chance, you will receive feedback for those items you needed anyway. There is a difference between a top-rated seller and top-rated plus. You need to become a top-rated seller to be able to even offer top-rated plus on your listings. Once you become a top-rated plus seller, you have the option to offer top-rated plus on any listings that you wish. That being said, I recommend that you only offer top-rated plus on any items that weigh under 1lb, or that are brand new and still pretty light. You have to offer free returns on the listing that you choose to offer top-rated plus on. This will reduce your profits, if you offer top-rated plus on heavy or even slightly damaged items. Don't even try. If you think an item has a high chance of a potential return, don't offer it, for example, if it has writing on the tag. According to eBay's official website, top-rated plus items: offer a minimum 30-day money-back return policy, Sellers commit to shipping the items in 1 business day with tracking provided, all items are from experienced sellers with the highest buyer ratings. As I previously mentioned always ship items within 1 business day, regardless of the platform. This will increase your sales. Who wants to order something that they will receive in 2 weeks? NO ONE. Always think like you're the consumer.

If you have a monopoly on an item, you can demand a higher price then you probably thought. If it doesn't sell fast, constantly drop it slightly, but be sure to still make a profit. If you have a monopoly on an item, and the item has lots of watchers (8+), you can safely raise the price. On eBay, you will get lots of questions from potential buyers, always be honest and answer fast. The worst part is that the people that ask questions usually don't end up purchasing the item or any others from you. You want to always offer exceptional service and the cheapest price on the platform you are selling on, or in many cases the cheapest on the whole internet. Always include packing slips at the beginning, write a little thank you note on them. Politely ask for good feedback. Feedback is everything on eBay! This is very important: Remember this "The pictures are the most important factor in selling any product". Offer best offers on all your items, this will give you a boost in traffic. Don't set a price limit, simply just decline the buyer's offers, if they are too low for you to make a profit.

Few people know how to generate money for themselves, fewer know to keep their hard-earned money, and fewer know how to multiply their money. - Oliver Petrik

Platform #2 Amazon

Amazon is the number #1 e-commerce platform by far. In terms of revenue, traffic, and sales. I personally don't sell on Amazon, because I have lots of used items. To sell on Amazon, you will need new items. Lots of them. The same concepts or strategies that you will utilize on eBay you will utilize on Amazon. The only main difference is the fee structure, and that you can't sell many types of used items on Amazon. Amazon is amazing if you have new products! eBay charges a 10% Final Value Fee plus promoted listing fees and PayPal fees. Amazon sellers receive their funds from their sales two weeks after the sales. Amazon sellers can choose two different selling plans: Professional or Individual. Individual sellers pay $0.99 for each item sold on Amazon, in addition to variable closing fees ranging from $0.45 to $1.35. Professional sellers pay variable closing fees and referral fee percentages ranging from 6% to 25% (an average of 13%). Professional sellers also pay $39.99 per month but are exempt from the $0.99 per item fee. If you plan on selling more than 40 products a month then the Professional Seller Program is a no-brainer for you. The main benefit of selling on Amazon is FBA (fulfilled by Amazon). You probably have seen endless ads on the internet for people teaching how to do FBA, it's very simple. Sellers who choose to participate in FBA delegate everything from fulfillment, packaging, sorting, and shipping to Amazon. This is very good for new sellers, sellers with endless inventory, or even sellers with limited space in their home or office. Whether you choose to sell on eBay, Amazon, or another platform depends solely on the products you have, and the business model you run. You can look up profit margins directly on the Amazon selling app, just by scanning UPC codes in stores. It will tell you the margins for fulfillment by you (the seller) or by FBA (Amazon).

Platform #3 Mercari and Poshmark

Mercari has quickly become my favorite selling platform. Even though I get much fewer sales on Mercari than I do on eBay, I like it because it is very simple, especially for beginners. Mercari charges a low commission of a flat 10% fee. That is it. Mercari fees are less than on Amazon or eBay. Mercari is also very easy to list products on. You can list on Mercari from either your phone or computer. One of the cons of Mercari is that you only have 40 characters available for the title. On Mercari, you want to price items a little higher than you want to sell them for and then drop them gradually. This is because you do not have the option to promote your listings on Mercari. Items get a boost in results only when you drop the price. So, price high, and gradually reduce the price. Another con with Mercari is that you have to wait to get paid until the buyer rates you, and you rate the buyer. However, this ensures that you will gather a lot of feedback fast. Each transaction gets you feedback or a rating on Mercari - guaranteed. If the buyer forgets to leave you a rating, Mercari does it automatically after a few days. Another con with Mercari compared to eBay is that they don't allow you to sell internationally. But sell on Mercari, I love it! It will definitely boost your income.

I am not too familiar with Poshmark, as I have never sold on it. But I researched it, and all platforms are very similar to each other. Poshmark was designed as a social selling and buying network. It is easy to list on Poshmark similar to Mercari. And there are no returns on either Mercari or Poshmark, this is very nice! I recommend that you pick either Mercari or Poshmark depending on the categories that you sell, and either Amazon or eBay. I haven't elaborated too much on either Mercari, Amazon or Poshmark for a reason. It's all pretty much the same, just minor differences. The sourcing aspect of your business is the most important, not the different platforms.

Here are some examples of platform combinations that I recommend. Research your items and always make informed and educated decisions. Any of my information described in this booklet isn't set in stone, do additional research and then act on that. Be sure to not cross-list or cross-post on more than two platforms at once with the same item.

Sell ON

eBay and Amazon

eBay and Mercari

eBay and Poshmark

Amazon and Mercari

Amazon and Poshmark

eBay and Mercari and Poshmark

ALL ABOUT
PACKAGING!

How should you package items? Well, obviously it depends on the item size and shape. Always package sold items using the safest, smallest, and lightest method possible. This means package it very securely, you do not want items to shift in their box during the shipment process. We all know the postal workers throw every little thing around. If there is extra room in the box around the item, throw in some tissue paper, clean plastic grocery bags, or anything to get rid of that extra room. This will reduce shifting during shipment. Stuffed animals or anything similar that is small and not fragile can be packaged in an envelope, but always surround them with either tissue paper or a grocery bag. Anything fragile always goes in a box. Anything in a box always goes in a box. Yes, any product that has a box, always goes in a box. Package stuff so it arrives at your customer's home, safely and intact, and not damaged, but also be as cost-efficient as possible. To do so, you have to keep both the weight and the dimensions of the package very low.

HOW TO LIST (THE RIGHT WAY)

The way you decide to list your items is very important, if you want to generate lots of sales. Of course, the item's photos are very important. Photos are just as important as the title. This is because they generate lots of attention. The order of the title is also very important. You should be titling items in this order (Condition, Brand, Size, Item, Details). For example: New Pixar Toy Story 4 10" Plush Woody the Cowboy Rare Vintage 2000. List in this manner or something very similar to it. Websites like Mercari only give you 40 characters for the title. For websites that do that, just include the brand, size, and item in your title. You don't have room to put anything in addition to that. However, always put words until you completely run out of characters. Always include item details in the description (as many as possible). eBay gives you lots of space for important item details. Mercari also gives you space for important item details, but it is dependent on the type of item. Always offer free shipping, and one business day or same day handling time on all of your items. (I have previously mentioned this, this is very important in order to generate lots of sales)

ALL ABOUT SHIPPING!

All About Shipping! Shipping and packaging go hand in hand with each other. Here's the order of shipping services that you should utilize if you live in the United States. 1. USPS MEDIA MAIL 2. USPS FIRST CLASS MAIL. 3. USPS PRIORITY MAIL. On Mercari, once you enter the weight of the item, it will tell you the different available services. PICK THE CHEAPEST ONE, unless that shipping company is very far away from you. Again, ask local businesses and friends and family for boxes and envelopes, or order them online. Make sure the item is very secure in its packaging and that it will not be damaged. If you use Mercari and have heavy items, I recommend using UPS, it is usually the cheapest. I very rarely use FedEx for anything.

RETURNS AND REFUNDS

Returns and Refunds! Try to avoid these at all costs! The only way, you can avoid them is, to be honest at all times, and reliable. If a buyer wants a return, maybe offer them a partial refund and the opportunity to keep the item. Whatever makes the most financial sense regarding your business, you always want to do.

TAXES!

Taxes! Only stupid people support high taxes. They slow the economy and GDP. I am currently writing a book about the benefits of Capitalism and government deregulation. Be on the lookout for that. It will be out sometime soon. The worst part about taxes is that you must comply with them, or you get punished. So be sure to understand your country's and jurisdiction's tax laws and also the rules for taxes on the platforms that you sell on. On eBay, you need to meet both of these selling requirements: over $20,000 in sales and over 200 transactions in a calendar year. Once you meet these requirements, PayPal will send you a tax form. Be sure to understand your country's and jurisdiction's tax laws and also the rules for taxes on the different platforms that you sell on. Comply with taxes. If you want to reduce them, vote for the best political candidate for that in your country or area.

RESELLER LANGUAGE (SLANG)

Reseller Slang!

EUC= Excellent Used Condition

EC= Excellent Condition

NWT= New with Tags

NWOT= New without the Tags

BEST OFFERS
OR OFFERS

eBay allows you to offer "best offers". Mercari allows "offers". Lots of platforms allow you to give your customers slight discounts on the listed price. I recommend offering best offer on all of your eBay listings. You can always reject them. You will receive lots of low balls, just reject them. Add a nice message and explain to the potential customer, why you cannot accept it. They understand. You run a business. Just use common sense when it comes to best offers. Whatever is in your best interest, do it! Do not utilize the auto reject best offer option on eBay, this is horrible. It will ruin your business. You will miss out on lots of sales including international ones.

<u>CONCLUSION!</u>

I hope you learned a lot from this booklet. I hope it opened your mind to all of the many endless possibilities with e-commerce, and some strategies that you need in order to become successful with e-commerce. The world of E-Commerce doesn't care if you are ugly, pretty, white, black, gay, straight, educated, or not, or anything in between. What E-Commerce actually rewards is dedication, honesty, hard work, and talent! Go out and make some money! I thank you for reading this booklet! Your purchase of this booklet benefited both you and me, that's the beauty of free markets and capitalism. NOW GO EXECUTE!